$\mathcal{L}$OVESPELLS

The AUTHENTIC Collection
of a WHITE WITCH

D1422826

LOVESPELLS

The AUTHENTIC Collection
of a WHITE WITCH

CLAIRE NAHMAD

Illustrations by JULIETTE PEARCE

PAVILION

To DIANNE BRAMHAM, *counsellor and wisewoman,*
this book is dedicated

☆

First published in 1993 by
PAVILION BOOKS LIMITED
196 Shaftesbury Avenue,
London WC2H 8JL

Text copyright © 1993 Claire Nahmad
Illustrations copyright © 1993 Juliette Pearce

Designed by Peter Luff

A CIP catalogue record for this book is available
from the British Library

ISBN 1-85145-9731

Printed and bound in Portugal

2 4 6 8 10 9 7 5 3 1

CONTENTS

EDITOR'S NOTE

☆

The material in this collection has been drawn from the
wisdom and teachings of my great-grandmother and her
daughter and namesake, Sarah Greaves. Born in the
nineteenth century in the old West Riding of Yorkshire,
both were known locally as "wisewomen" – figures who
possessed a fund of native wisdom, herb-healing and other
special powers which they used to help others.

☆

My inheritance from both Sarahs has produced the
following book. The spells it contains are true to the spirit
of country lore and those deeper folk beliefs passed down
from generation to generation. They represent a tradition in
which inspiration for healing, human relationships, the
lover's art and magic, has ever been the domain of women.

☆

Claire Nahmad

INTRODUCTION

☆

This collection of spells, taken from the handwritten
manuscripts of a genuine white witch, represents
a fascinating element in British folklore tradition; one which
gives intimations, whispered and sublime, of a time long
ago when country people lived close to the earth
and moved consciously and observantly through the cyclic
rhythm of the seasons.

☆

These people understood the magic of natural things and
the divinity, the sacred heart, that was inherent in
them – that living spirit which blesses the lives and human
purposes of those who can respond to it with
sensitivity, creativity and reverence.

☆

To such people of ages past, and especially to the white
witches, or "wisewomen", living at their midst
who taught the secrets of magical thinking, Christianity and
wiselore were by no means incompatible – rather
they were considered as complementary to one another.

☆

The birth of the Christ Child as the Celtic "son of light" is
celebrated in the depths of midwinter when darkness
and death in the outer world hold nature in thraldom; the
winter solstice is at its peak; no life stirs in the ground.
Then, miraculously, the sun turns from his declining
course, the days grow longer and the life-force in
nature reasserts itself; the babe of hope is born again and
becomes the young and vigorous child of light and
life which is the incoming spring. This marvellous birth
takes place after the shortest, darkest day of the
dying year – and so occurs the Christ Mass, the celebration
of the light (the word "Christ" means "the true light").

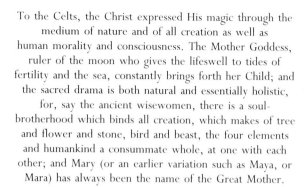

To the Celts, the Christ expressed His magic through the medium of nature and of all creation as well as human morality and consciousness. The Mother Goddess, ruler of the moon who gives the lifeswell to tides of fertility and the sea, constantly brings forth her Child; and the sacred drama is both natural and essentially holistic, for, say the ancient wisewomen, there is a soul-brotherhood which binds all creation, which makes of tree and flower and stone, bird and beast, the four elements and humankind a consummate whole, at one with each other; and Mary (or an earlier variation such as Maya, or Mara) has always been the name of the Great Mother.

☆

This, then, is the philosophy behind these spells; a living and simple philosophy, beautiful in its application, and relevant to our times: anyone who loves the earth and deplores the way our alienated modern society treats her, can hardly fail to respond to its teaching.

☆

Perhaps it is time for the ancient wisdom at the very roots of our being to make its triumphal march back into our lives! To study and to use these spells is to turn again to nature and to the mysticism which informs and complements it; to nurture a sense of wonder and of magic as we contemplate stars and flowering herbs and branches in leaf and the full shining moon; to listen to our dreams and the quiet voice of our inner selves, that they may yield their wisdom and their vision.

☆

Perhaps, too, there is a deep truth underlying the fact that the spells deal with divinatory revelations concerning romantic love and marriage! . . . for the love which overcomes and transcends the duality bisecting nature is the mystery at the heart of creation.

8

Of MAIDENS
& the MOON

Through countless ages, the moon has been regarded as a
beautiful symbol of the mother aspect of the Godhead – an
emblem of the Mother Goddess.

☆

For all magical workings, it is necessary to attune
yourself to the moon; look for her in the early evening
skies as night draws on (sometimes she rises before the
daylight is gone). Contemplate her mystery, her beauty, the
majesty and magnetism of her serene shining. Do not be
afraid to commune with the moon, for meditation upon her
will unveil many deep secrets.

☆

The mysterious Ceridwen, goddess of the Celts, is
associated with the moon. Presiding over her
magic cauldron, she dispenses life and death to humanity –
a poetical symbol of the moon's tides of abundance and
withdrawal and their effect upon the life-forces of the earth
and her bodies of water. Ceridwen is the daughter of the
Dagda, the great Celtic god who is father of humankind
and whose magical harp charms into being the eternal
round of the seasons, which again suggests the influence of
the moon, as she measures the months or "moonths" of
the yearly cycle. Although Celtic mythology identifies them
as father and daughter, a deeper interpretation intimates
that they are the masculine and feminine principles of the
one supreme Godhead honoured by the Celts.

Traditionally, Astarte is "the moon with crescent horns"; Hecate represents the invisible moon; and Selene or Luna, who fell in love with the sleeping Endymion, the full moon. The white witch, however, eschews conventional mythology to some extent, for the sake of her own magical purposes. There are five phases of the moon which concern the working of these spells.

☆

First comes the new moon, also called the Bride's moon. The word "bride" came into our language from ancient echoes of the Celtic goddess Brigit or Brigid, who ruled the moon and presided over hearth and home. (She later became St Bridget. Closely associated with womanhood, she was goddess of the moon, of lovers, and of the fiery stars, which perhaps explains why she was also the goddess of inspiration and poetry.) This is followed by the waxing moon, which is the moon of Diana the Huntress; the full moon, which is the moon of Artemis or Freya; the waning moon, which is Hecate's moon; and, finally, the dark of the moon – the night or nights after the final waning of Hecate when no moon is visible in the heavens. This last phase is the time of the Morrigan, the Nights of Morgana, and no magic should be worked on these days.

☆

When the moon is waxing to full, choose spells which directly relate to the moon. When she is waning towards the time of the Morrigan, the remaining spells can be tried. There is no hard and fast rule; but during the time of the waxing and full moon, you will be drawing power towards you, and as the moon wanes you will be banishing what is undesired away from your sphere of operation.

☆

The moon is the maiden's ally in matters of the heart: make her your friend.

The KALE Marriage Spell

☆

This is an old Yorkshire spell which maidens in the north
country have favoured for many long years.

☆

Wait for a waxing moon; then go outdoors and stand up on
something like a box or chair which you have never
used for the purpose before. You will bear with you a dish
of cold kale, which you must hold in the moonlight and
ask the moon to bless. This being done, you must say aloud:

☆

"Hot kale or cold kale, I drink thee
For moon-touched and magic you be;
If ever I marry a man or a man marry me
I ask that this night I may him see;
And tomorrow may him ken
In church or market above all other men."

☆

You must then drink nine times, and, having done so, leave
the rest in the dish as homage to the moon. Bow in
great devotion to her, and when you are in your chamber,
you must go to bed backwards. Then you will see
in your dreams the man you are to marry, and may expect
to recognize the earthly counterpart of your vision
soon at church, in the market square, or yet at the next
country fair.

The DRUID'S MOON *Spell*

☆

This spell must be worked when the moon is full, and in those seasons when it can truly be called a Druid's moon – that is, when the features of a fair young maiden in her first girlhood can be seen plainly masking the moon's face, bearing a garland of oak-leaves upon her brow. This is the true Druid's moon.

☆

Gather by moonlight nine pebbles, grey or white, and take them to a hilltop (a mound or hillock will serve just as well). Form a ring with the stones and build a little fire within it. Burn dried lavender and pine-cones in its flames, and gaze long upon the moon. As the incense rises, intone these words:

☆

"Magic moon, magic moon,
Shod me with your silver shoon,
Answer what I ask tonight
And I'll dance by your fair light."

☆

Having chanted the rune, you must dance upon the hilltop as the moon inspires, until you are weary, meditating all the while upon the question in your heart which you would ask of the moon – its nature should be of love and marriage, of riches, or of some project which you wish to undertake.

☆

Dance whilst the fire dies down; and then when the ashes are cool, take the stones encircling them and form a cross in their midst. Gather some of the ashes and put them in your handkerchief, and shake a pinch into each shoe. Then hurry home, slip under your pillow the handkerchief you carry, and place your shoes together under the bed,

14

climbing into it immediately afterwards. Before noon the next day, go again to the place where you worked the spell, and examine the cross of stones with great care. If it is just as you left it, perfect and undisturbed, the answer to your question is as you should wish it to be; but if any one of the stones should be displaced, then you must accept your disappointment with resignation.

The NIGHTINGALE
LOVE-IN-MOURNING *Spell*
(A spell to bind and heal a broken heart)

☆

Find a little wood or a spinney where the nightingale gives
forth her lovely notes in the shade of the evening,
and go there dressed in white muslin. Gather wild roses
pink and white. Pin them in your bosom with a brooch
of silver. Find a fairy ring (which is a circle of grass of a

richer, deeper green where the fairies make their revels), or, if you cannot, make a magic circle by walking three times round a grassy space sunwise. Stand or sit, according to your comfort, in the middle of it and wait for the moon to rise, keeping within the boundary of your magic ring. As soon as you hear the song of the nightingale, you must spread the roses you have plucked around your feet, and dance in measured and rhythmical steps, taking care not to trample on the roses, and chanting as you dance three times over:

☆

"Pretty bird, fairy bird,
Your song you sing without a word;
In ancient language clear and sweet
My broken heart you softly greet.
With all my soul I wish you may
Charm my heart's distress away."

☆

Then you must return to the centre of the circle, and sit awhile in perfect silence, contemplating the serenity of the moon and the stars. Lastly, gather again the roses you have scattered and make a little shrine of them in the centre of the magic ring. If dew has fallen upon them, that is all the better.

☆

You must dedicate them to St Rita, who is the Saint of Broken Hearts and Thwarted Desires, and say a prayer of thanksgiving over them. Take from the consecrated pile one white rose and one pink rose, and place them under your pillow. You will surely wake to find that sweet comfort has cheered your sad sorrow and given you heart's ease.

The PRAYER BOOK *Marriage Spell*

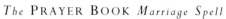

☆

This is a spell to try during the shining of the harvest
moon. Spend some moments before going to bed standing
quietly in contemplation of its splendour, and if you
conveniently may, let this be out of doors and alone, in the
garden or a wild place.

☆

On retiring, place beneath your pillow a worn and mellow
prayer book, open at the page in the wedding service
containing the words "With this ring I thee wed"; place
upon the page a ring, a key, a fragrant herb, a
garden flower, a tender sprig of green willow, a small
heart-cake, a crust of fresh-baked bread and the
following cards: ace of diamonds, ace of spades, ten of
clubs and nine of hearts, Enfold all these in a delicate
handkerchief of muslin or gauze.

As you creep beneath the bed-linen, repeat this rune three times out loud:

☆

"Luna, every woman's friend,
To me thy goodness condescend;
Let me this night in visions see
Emblem of my destiny."

☆

Now if you dream of storms, of graveyards, or a plunging moonlit sea, sorrow and troubles await you, which you must determine to pass through with a staunch heart; if of a ring, or snow-white swans in flight, or yet the ace of diamonds, passion, courtship and marriage will occur soon in your life; if of a willow, or a troop of wood-elves, or the wind shaking tree-tops, that is a warning of treachery and loss and vanishing expectations; and should wild geese appear in your dreams, you will marry more than once.

The RIBBON *Marriage Spell*

☆

Now this proceeding is to be followed during the time of Hecate's moon, which is her waning. It is to be essayed at night, in the secret hours after midnight, and on a clear night, so that the stars are out and the old moon burns like a dim candle, for you will need her light to work by.

☆

Take two long and identical strips of ribbon, red as hearts. Fold over each strip of ribbon so that both are doubled and their ends meet. Use a piece of scarlet silk to join the two doubled ribbons neatly at the point where the crease is made in doubling them; now the conjoined ribbons will display four ends. Upon that crease must be fastened a wedding ring borrowed from an elderly matron. You must also steal away your sweetheart's scarf-pin or ring, or another piece of personal jewellery, for a little while, so that it can be secured in the wall outside the window of your bedchamber.

☆

Hang the ribbon upon the scarf-pin or piece of jewellery, in the form of a holy cross, against the wall, fastening its four arms in place with pins.

☆

Now retire to your bed and do not approach your window until three hours after the sun's rising. If, on studying the ribbons after the prescribed number of hours have passed by, you see that any of them have faded or altered in colour, you are fated not to be joined in wedlock with your present sweetheart; but if their colours remain fast and unchanged, that shows that of a surety you will soon be happily married to him.

The OWL *Lovespell*

☆

Now when the moon is waxing and the spirit of Diana rides high, the night owls love to call to one another across the gloomy moonlit distances. If a young maid wishes to know her fortune in love, she should frame her question clearly in her mind's eye, and seek out a lonely place in the woods on such a night as is described above.

☆

She must put each of her questions to the owls; and if they hoot once whilst she counts off nine on her fingers, the answer is yes; and if they call twice as she does the same, the answer is no. Should it be that the owls call three times during her counting, then the answer is open to question, and may be swayed by her actions hereafter.

☆

To hear the owls call in the time of the Morrigan, when there is no moon, is a disturbing sign; for it presages a tide of events haunted by troubles and sorrow, and a struggle must be entered upon to ensure that all things should work together for good.

The ACORN Lovespell

☆

Now work this spell under the goodly radiance of a full moon, for it is a Druid spell. It may be essayed in any of the months between September and March, and if it can be done on the third or the ninth instance of the month, then that is all the better.

☆

Any odd number of maidens, not exceeding nine, must gather together, and keep grave and solemn countenances. Each one of you must take a piece of string and nine acorns. Pierce the hearts of the acorns and thread them on to the string. Now you must gather around the fire and every maid burn three of the hairs from her head.

☆

When this is done, bring forth a long slender twig and bind the string of nine acorns around it, each maid playing her part so that all have a brand to place upon the fire.

☆

Wait for the church clock to strike midnight, and precisely upon the hour you must all consign your sacrifices to the flames. Unbroken silence must be maintained throughout, or the spell will die.

☆

The company of maidens must stand around the fire and watch it consume the acorns and fall into embers. Then the ashes must be removed and scattered outside on to the night. You must go directly to bed, chanting this rune addressed to Cupid in unison as you mount the stairs:

☆

"May love and marriage be the theme
To visit me in this night's dream;
Fire and moon and sacred oak
Your threefold power we thus invoke;

22

Be all three my faithful friend
The image of my lover send;
Let me see his form and face
And his occupation trace
By a symbol or a sign;
Cupid, forward my design."

OLD-MOON-IN-A-MIST *Lovespell*

☆

When the old moon rises in a mist, knowledgeable old
wives predict that troubles will soon rain on true lovers.
To ward off the maleficence, you must bow three times
to the moon and intone:

☆

*"Old Mother, Old Mother, blink clear your eye;
So no tears shall be shed for my lover and I."*

The APPLE *Marriage Spell*

☆

Wait for the night of Bride's moon, which is the new
moon's pretty crescent. Stand before her at an
open window, and pare an apple with a golden sheen so
that the skin is whole. Throw the peel over your left
shoulder, and it will take the shape of the initial letter of
that name your future husband will bear.

The TEACUP *Spell*

☆

You must settle yourself down with a hot cup of tea
and drink it slowly, thinking pleasant, calm thoughts all the
while. When the cup is nigh on empty, wave it thrice
round your head with the hand you used in drinking it, and
turn it upside down upon the saucer. Then, on taking
it up, you will see how the tea-leaves lie within the cup. If
they are gathered deep and thick and mostly all at the
bottom, you will be married in a twelvemonth, you will be
happy and prosper, and have as many children as you
desire. If the tea-leaves cluster mainly about the side of the
cup nearest the handle, you will have many good friends
and allies; but if the leaves cling in their greatest number to
the opposite side of the cup, you must count the number
of leaves, or groups of leaves, so scattered about to
calculate the number of years which are destined to elapse
before your wedding-day.

☆

Young maidens will find that the prognostics of this spell
are most accurate if it is worked as a full moon is rising.

SAINTS, STAR
GODDESSES, &
the SUNSET *of*
OLD TALES

Many of the spells in this collection are dedicated to
saints and the eve of their celebratory days. It may seem
surprising that lovespells, dreaming and nature magic –
which many might regard as the superstitious practices of a
primitive country people – should be associated with
saints of the orthodox Christian Church!

☆

What happened was that as the Celtic beliefs of the old
world fused with incoming Christianity, the names of
the old gods and goddesses were superseded by those of the
saints of the new religion; but whilst their names were
displaced, the spiritual truths which they symbolized were
not. As the new religion took hold in Britain the process of
adapting was simply a matter of gaining a fresh perspective,
a more evolved perspective, on existing knowledge. The
later Celts saw magic and mystery in the world through the
medium of visionary Christianity, and their charms,
spells, prayers and blessings testify to a beautiful and deeply
spiritual understanding of the religion, potent with wonder
and marvels, which is far removed from the orthodox
and fundamentalist approach.

. . . And so St Michael supersedes Llew, the god of the sun; Ceridwen, the goddess of nature and the mysteries of life and death, presiding over her magic cauldron, becomes St Catherine. The mother goddesses of fertility, Ma and Matrona, became St Mary, and their names passed into our culture as names for mother figures; and, as we have already seen, the goddess Brigit or Brigid, who ruled the moon and the stars and presided over hearth and home, became St Bridget, while in her other aspect as Goddess of Love she also became St Agnes.

☆

Looking up into the night sky, we find that the stars pay eternal tribute to the memory of the star goddesses. Arianrhad the mother goddess gave her name to what we now know as the Corona Borealis and the Milky Way. The constellation Cassiopeia was once known as Lys Dôn, meaning the Court of the Children of Dôn (from Danu, Great Mother of fertility, learning and culture).

☆

There are numerous folk tales of lost kingdoms beneath the sea, with bells that can sometimes be heard as they swing in the tide. In the same way the old gods seem to have sunk beneath the waves of our consciousness, yet live on in myth and magic. Hidden in the depths of our being, they call to us sometimes with haunting bell-like voices of a beauty that is long gone, but rediscoverable, if we will only unfetter our imagination a little.

☆

So this is the mystery behind the spells of the saints; their earthly lives as sainted men and women are celebrated; yet beyond the human story stretches the sea of Celtic myth, and the enchanted western isles.

First Star of the Evening *Lovespell*

☆

Look for the first star of the evening, which will generally
be Mercury or Venus. Imagine that there is a little star
shining in your own heart like those which jewel the
firmament. Let your heart fill up with starlight, even so
that it shines from your eyes. You will then perform the
dance of the stars, outside on a grassy place. Ask me not
how this is to be done, for the stars themselves will tell it
to you. If you are not joyous, the spell is not worked.

Then go to your bedchamber directly, and intone this rune
to the Evening Star:

☆

"Gentle Venus, be my friend
My heart's true love I bid you send."

☆

You will then drink from a crystal wineglass a measure of
the Venus Love Elixir, which is a liquid consisting of boiled
water, pink rose petals and a single thimbleful of honey.
Let this stand by your bed ready and waiting for you, and
after you have imbibed, settle down to sleep. Once you
have performed this spell three times on three different
nights, you cannot help but draw your true love to you like
a magnet, even though he be unknown to you.

The DREAMING CAKE *Lovespell*

☆

On St Faith's day, which falls on 6th October, it is the
custom for young damsels to make the "Dumb Cake", or
"Dreaming Cake", in a mystical ceremony.

☆

Now the number of the party never exceeds three; they
meet in silence to make the cake, which is to be of
honey and oats and other good natural things; as soon as
the clock strikes twelve, they each break a portion off
to eat; and when done, they walk up to bed backwards
without speaking a word, for if one of them makes any
murmur the spell is broken.

☆

Those maidens whose lovers are true (be they self-declared
or secret admirers) see the likeness of their
sweethearts hurrying after them, as if wishing to catch them
before they get into bed; but the maids, being apprized
of this beforehand by the cautions of old dames who have
tried it, take care to unpin their hair and loosen their
clothes before they start, and are ready to slip into bed
before they are caught by the pursuing shadow, thereby
avoiding the terror of such a situation.

☆

If nothing is seen, the desired token may be a knocking at
the doors or a loud rustling in the house, as soon as they
have retired. To be convinced that it comes from nothing
else but the spell's magic, they are always particular in
turning out the cats and dogs before the ceremony begins.

☆

Those whose swains are untrue and who are deceived, or
who are to die unmarried, neither see nor hear
anything; but they are sure to dream terrible dreams, of
new-made graves, winding sheets and lonely churchyards

ghastly in moonlight, and of rings that will fit no finger, or
if they do, crumble and fall away into dust as soon as
they are put on; whereas the dreams of the lucky maidens
will be rosy and sweet.

St Catherine's Eve *Lovespell*

☆

In order to work this spell on St Catherine's Eve, which
falls on 24th November, you need two friends to assist
you. It should be tried directly after eating the first egg laid
by a pullet or young hen. You also need to have a Bible
and a key laid out ready: be sure that the key is long
enough to protrude at both the bottom and the top of the
leaves of the Bible. Place the key over the famous words of
Ruth, chapter five, verse sixteen: "Entreat me not to leave
thee, or to return from following thee; for where thou
goest I will go, and where thou lodgest I will lodge; thy
people shall be my people, and thy God shall be my God."

☆

After the words have been intoned, the Bible is to be shut
and tied around with tape. The two accompanying friends
stretch out the forefingers of their left hands, and the maid
who is trying the spell suspends the Bible between them,
resting the protruding parts of the key upon their
respective forefingers. As she does so, she repeats the
words of Ruth, but this time inserting into the text her
own lover's name.

☆

If the key and the Bible do not balance but fall to the floor,
the answer of the oracle is in her favour. If the Bible
and the key remain suspended, her wishes in love will not
be granted. If this be so, the fair damsel may still rejoice,
though she also sorrows; for she may be sure that the lover
of her desires would not have made her happy; and another
lover will be assigned to her by providence.

The DOVE'S EGG
& EARLY TULIP *Lovespell*

☆

Upon St Mark's Eve, 25th April, take a dove's egg and
hard-boil it; eat it whole with salt and springwater, taking
care to bury the shell in the garden afterwards.

☆

The pretty Early Tulip with its fiery hues is sacred to St
Mark, so as you retire in perfect silence to your chamber
after the ceremony of burying the dove's egg, you must take
one of these flowers with you and keep it at your bedside
in a glass of water. The spell being now complete, your
lover will come to you in your dreams. Upon the morrow,
wear the tulip all day in homage to good St Mark.

ST MARK'S EVE *Marriage Spell*

☆

This spell is to be worked on 25th April, St Mark's Eve.
Young ladies seeking marriage will do well to work their
spells on certain honoured days of the year, which include
the eves and vigils of the saints.

☆

An old charm says:

☆

"On St Mark's Eve at twelve o'clock
Let the fair maid watch her smock;
She'll find her husband in the dark
By praying unto good St Mark."

☆

The smock is placed on a chair before the fire. The maid
waits alone in the silent room to watch the shadows
fall. Her bridegroom-to-be will appear as the dusk closes in
and the dew falls in the garden, the smock magically
assuming his shape.

The MAY DEW *Spell*

☆

Should any maid tiptoe from her bed and go out alone
at sunrise on May Day, and bathe in the blessed May dew
which bediamonds the flowers and the grass in a meadow,
she will be fair of face and lovely all year round, and will
have many eager and loving swains as suitors.

The BEDPOST & GARTER *Lovespell*

☆

Upon St Mark's Eve, let a young damsel tie her garter
nine times round the bedpost, and knit nine knots in it,
intoning the while:

☆

"This knot I knit, this knot I tie,
To see my love as he goes by,
In his apparel and array
As he walks in every day."

☆

Then she will see her true love in a dream.

36

The COMPANY OF GHOSTS
Marriage Spell

☆

If you be stout of heart, then on St Mark's Eve, go in the
evening to the church-porch; lay there the branch
of a rowan tree, or else a full-blown rose, of a size to be
readily found in the dark, and then return home to
await the approach of midnight. Proceed to the porch again
before the clock strikes twelve, with as many as you
choose to accompany you, and be sure to remain there till
the clock has struck. Your companions must fetch again
the flower or branch you left in the porch as far as the
church-gate. Let them reach this gate before twelve,
and before the clock begins to strike; and there let them
wait for you in silence.

☆

You must stay in the church-porch alone.

☆

On the stroke of midnight, if you are to be married,
expect to see a marriage-procession pass you by, with a
bride in your own likeness hanging on to the arm of the
shade of your future husband. As many bridesmen and
maidens as appear to follow them, so many months or
years will you have to wait for marriage.

☆

If you are to die unmarried, then the ghostly procession
will be of a funeral, consisting of a coffin covered
in a snow-white sheet, borne on the shoulders of shadows
that seem without heads, and followed by mourners
who weep and sigh.

The BOUQUET *Lovespell*

☆

Try this spell upon the Eve of St John, whose feast day is
Midsummer's Day. Fair young damsels must gather a
selection of flowers to make up the bouquet: camomile,
which you will know by its feathery green leaves, its
white-eyed daisies, and its apple-like scent; sweet violets
from the woods, and that lovely flower called the yellow
archangel; and, lastly, St John's wort, highest in significance
amongst the other flowers. This herb you may recognize
by its cluster of flowers golden as evening sunlight, which,
when pressed between your fingers, give forth a juice
blood-red. Gather your flowers from nine different places.

The bouquet is to be placed under the maiden's pillow
at midnight, bound around with a little piece of pure white
lace. Its delightful fragrance will steal into your
deepest dreaming hours and bring you visions of your true
love, whoever he is destined to be.

A VALENTINE'S DAY
Spell for Betrothal

☆

Old tales tell of a spell which is to be used thus on St
Valentine's Day: take five bay leaves, and pin four of them
in the four corners of your pillow, and the fifth at
its centre; as you lie down to prepare for sleep, you must
repeat this charm seven times, counting up to seven, seven
times over, between each repetition (mark the numbers
off on your fingers for the sake of accuracy):

☆

"Sweet Guardian Angel, let me have
What I most earnestly do crave –
A Valentine endued with love
Who will both true and constant prove."

☆

Your betrothed-to-be will afterwards appear to you in a
dream, and soon enough in real life.

☆

The yellow crocus is the flower which is dedicated to St
Valentine, and should be worn on his day upon the breast
of all true lovers, pinned over the heart.

Lovespell for the
FEAST DAY OF ST AGNES

☆

St Agnes is the tender-hearted saint for all young maidens
who are lovers, and they will do well to call on her upon
her feast day, which falls upon 21st January.

☆

On that day, and the very minute it begins, you must rise
up swiftly from your bed and stand at the church door
before one o'clock in the morning.

☆

Put the forefinger of your left hand into the keyhole of the
church door, and murmur over to yourself three times
three this simple rune:

☆

"O sweet St Agnes, now draw near,
With my true love straightway appear."

☆

Then return speedily to your bed, and before cockcrow
your lover will appear to you in a dream, in which he will
impart to you the secret of whether or not you are to be
bound in wedlock together.

☆

The flower which is known as the Christmas Rose is sacred
to the memory of the beautiful St Agnes, and one worn
in the breast all the day in her honour will foster the magic
of the spell. If, late in the evening, when you retire to rest
and are about to lay your head upon your pillow, you
place the flower which you have lifted from your breast so
that it lies beneath your hair, the working of this ancient
spell will be made more potent.

A MAY DAY *Marriage Spell*

☆

This May Day marriage spell is sacred to St Mary, and is to be performed thus: Prepare a syllabub of fresh milk from a brown cow and rosehip wine in a capacious vessel; take a golden wedding ring, ask Mother Mary to bless it, and drop it into the concoction, observing solemn ceremony. A party of fair maids shall now draw lots as to who shall first try to dip out the wedding ring with a ladle; and so you take turns and as you meet with success, so shall you in that wise be wed – the first maid to be victorious is the first one to be married, and the last to triumph is the last to be married. Should any one of you fail at your third turn, try no more; for it is your fate to remain in the single state, at least for many years to come.

Of Candles
& Mirror
Magic

When we observe the still reflection of a star in a puddle
of water, we witness a miracle. The star may be
considerably larger than our own earth, it may be many
light years distant; yet its image is faithfully imparted
to us by an ephemeral pool of water of perhaps no more
than a finger's depth.

☆

There is a magic in this; when we consider the shallowness
of our own mortal lives and the transiency of our personal
life-span in comparison with eternity, it would not perhaps
be too far-fetched to liken ourselves to puddles! The
point is, in our puny mortal being, we too can reflect stars.

☆

The deep mystery of the magic of mirrors and their
principle of reflection has ever been a source of fascination.
They occur again and again in folk and fairy tales dating
back to furthest antiquity. In ancient Egypt the spirit of the
mirror was Hathor, the goddess of wisdom; in Britain,
Morgana Le Fay, Queen of Witches, sought counsel from
her enchanted mirror. In its symbolism we may read that it
is a signature for the soul.

☆

Wiselore teaches that it is the soul's quality of stillness,
lending to it the capacity to reflect, which is its greatest

power; and as the moon reflects the rays of the sun, so the soul reflects the light which is at the heart of eternity, symbolized down the ages by the flame of the candle.

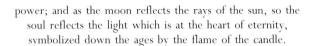

There is another point for contemplation in the way that the flame of the candle softens the rigid wax, making it pliable and malleable. In a similar way the burning of the light within ourselves empowers us to shape and mould our destiny and our lives according to inspiration and guidance from the spirit.

☆

In consideration of all this, it is not surprising that candles, mirrors and pools of water figure as magical tools and enchanted passports to mystical experience in this collection of lovespells and dreaming spells – if we understand mystical experience as meaning simple but deep communion with our secret inner selves rather than religious experience in a dogmatic or conventional sense.

☆

It is in this spirit that we may best explore these spells, and learn most from them, holding in our awareness the beauty of the meaning in these symbols and the radiant and tranquil wisdom of their teaching.

A Lovespell for WALPURGIS NIGHT

☆

As twilight falls on Walpurgis Night, the eve of May Day,
the maid should find a mandrake and draw a cross in the
soil, with the plant at the centre. Mark out the cross with
four candles, and light each one. If they should burn only
for a moment before being snuffed out by the wind, that is
enough; if they can be lit all together so that they illumine
the mandrake as they burn, that is very good.

Take up the mandrake with care. If you should hear its
strange cry, which is something like that of the keening
voice of the peewit, you know certainly that your future is
to be told. Study its root; if it resembles the figure of a
man, that is very lucky; but if the figure in the roots looks
like a woman, that is unlucky, and the mandrake oracle is
seeking to warn you of impending misfortune. For a young
man, naturally, the spell works the other way round.

☆

When you have done, put the mandrake back in the ground
with due solicitude, and bury your candles next to its
roots. So you will have a friend and protector until the
next year's Walpurgis Night.

HALLOWE'EN *Lovespell*

☆

This is a spell to be worked after dark on All Hallows Eve.
To obtain guidance in love, procure a basin of cold water
drawn from a well, and begin to melt a candle. Watch, and
ponder in your heart the question you wish to have
answered. When the candle has melted, drop the hot wax
into the basin of well water. You may judge of the answer
to your question concerning happiness and fulfilment
in love, or indeed any other matter, by reading the various
fantastic shapes and configurations the wax assumes.

☆

Read the symbols thus: if the wax forms a flower or the
shape of a bird, these are happy omens; if it should dispose
itself into the sculpture of an animal, consult your own
associations with that animal (a fox signifies cunning and
caution; a mole, some feeling or activity which is not being
declared; a hare, the signature of spring, new beginnings
and an omen of speedy and swift fulfilment to your plans; a
horse, a journey – and strength given to you to undertake
it; and a squirrel, life is storing a hoard of good things
for you). If you see a tree, expect to receive wisdom from
an elderly person and a place of harbour in distress; if
you see clouds, that betokens problems and suggests that
your heart and mind are not clear on the subject that you
contemplate; if you see a star, that is light in your
darkness; if you see a face, study its expression, whether
mournful, glad or pensive. Read the symbols by meditating
upon the wisdom in your own heart.

☆

You may ask three questions of the method, working the
same spell. Use it in the manner of a sacred oracle, wise
and instructive. So did the witches of old in these parts
disport themselves in divination, magic and craftworking.

46

WOOD, EARTH & WATER *Lovespell*

☆

Go to your bedchamber at the time of the full moon, and light two candles, pure and white, to make a little altar. Write the names of all your suitors upon bits of paper, then roll each one separately in a mite of potter's clay. Take a clear glass bowl filled with water from a spring, and drop the clay balls into it: the first that rises to the surface bears the name of your true love.

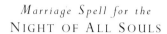

Marriage Spell for the
NIGHT OF ALL SOULS

☆

To work this spell upon the night of All Souls, 2nd
November, two single young men or two single young
women must venture out by candlelight, hand in
hand, to the cabbage or kale garden, and with eyes fast
closed must both uproot the first plant their fingers alight
on, taking one plant each. Its being well-formed or
crooked, large or small, is prophetic of the likeness of their
future spouse. They may search, too, for those signs and
significations in the shape of the plant which will whisper
more subtle predictions concerning the nature of
that marriage-partner; for example, leaves spread out wide
indicate generosity, whereas tightly closed leaves point
to an uncharitable nature.

☆

If soil clings to the root of the plant, that indicates you will
be the richer for marrying. The stem of the plant is then

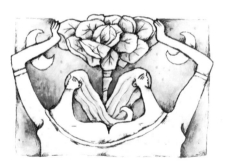

opened and its heart is tasted; and as the taste is bitter,
sweet or tart, so it is augured will be the disposition and
temper of the future spouse.

FRIDAY NIGHT *Dreaming Spell*

☆

An ancient rhyming proverb proclaims:

☆

"Friday night's dream
On Saturday told
Is sure to come true
Be it ever so old."

☆

Friday is consecrated to the goddess Freya (whose Celtic name was Bridget), who rules love and wisdom, women and the moon. Gentlemen like to think it is an unlucky day for them and their business, but it is most gracious to maidens and their concerns, and is goodly indeed for the working of dreaming spells.

☆

Try out your spells on a Friday, if you can, the best hour being that of six o'clock, or yet the eleventh hour. And remember, if a young maiden dreams upon a Friday night of a man who has won her heart and her fancy, and tells that dream to a bosom friend, the very next day, that of course being Saturday, she is very likely to wed with him. Anything that is inspirational, that has to do with love and the heart or contemplation of the future, is best done on a Friday, for it is a day that augurs fair for maidens; bear this in mind.

The ANGEL IN THE MIRROR *Lovespell*

☆

This spell bears a terrible solemnity in its purposes and
must never be essayed with casual intent.

☆

Light three white candles or, better still, silver ones if you
can procure them, and light them at the rising of the full
moon, having blessed the taper first by making the sign of
the cross on it. Chant this rune:

☆

"Angel of the Mirror, Angel of the Moon,
Grant to me your presence as a precious boon."

☆

Then take your candles and place them before a looking-
glass, one which you may sit at to gaze into its depths,
having made certain before beginning the working that it is
beautifully polished. Frame the question which is in your
heart to the candles and to the mirror, and wait awhile.

☆

Soon you will begin to perceive that a form is taking shape within the candle-lit mirror, although heretofore it reflected nothing but the shining candles, yourself, and images of the darkened room.

☆

If the figure which appears thus is that of a fair angel, all exquisite in shades and swirls of purest white, gentle silver and pearly moonlight, like unto a vision of peace, that is the Angel Gabriel, the angel of the moon, and the answer to your question is that which you most wished to hear. But if a dark lady appears, lovely and terrible and full of shadowy enchantment, hung with a dim veil as if it were made of raindrops falling at darkest midnight, then that is Morgana, the Dark Angel; she comes to warn you that what you desire must not be pursued.

☆

After working the spell, quickly put out the candles with your own breath and give thanks to that image in the mirror which appeared to you.

The LOOKING-GLASS *Marriage Spell*

☆

Young maids should inscribe their names on scraps of paper at midnight, afterwards burning them in the flame of a white candle, lit for the purpose, and then carefully gathering up the delicate ashes, which should be closely bound in rose petals of a pink and white hue.

Let them then take a looking-glass from their toilet-table, mark it with a cross, and cover its silver face with the rose petals; this they should slip under their pillow; and then they will see in their dreams the spouse upon whom they will bestow their hand and heart.

☆

Remember that the Lady Moon is the Mistress of Dreams and Mirrors, and you would do well to petition her respectfully beforehand.

New Year's Eve *Lovespell*

☆

Upon retiring to your chamber after the festivities of New Year's Eve, light a candle to the moon and ask her help in divination. As you go to bed, take a hand-mirror and a Bible, and wait for the stroke of one o'clock, which marks the passing of the first mystical hour of the year. Open up

the sacred volume, and place the mirror in its pages at random in the dark, having snuffed the candle as the clock began to strike. Lay the Bible at your bedside, and as soon as you awaken in the morning, take it up again and discover unto yourself which verses the mirror lies upon in the leaves of the holy book, taking care to note not only the area of the text the mirror covers on the right-hand page but also the corresponding area on the left-hand page. Study, then, both of the texts which the mirror in its wisdom has prescribed for your instruction; you will learn therein the secrets of the coming year, especially those concerned with love matters, the verses prophesying through symbols and significance the course of events.

The CANDLES & THE SPIRIT *Lovespell*

☆

Take a crystal bowl and fill it from a well, a spring or
a running stream, as you do so speaking an invocation to
the spirit of the waters to aid you in divination. Carry it
home and place it on a table in the dark, setting around it
nine candles which you will light with a blessed taper.

☆

Now put your question to the spirit in the water. If
the answer is no, and the young man in your heart is to be
denied you, the water spirit which some call the Kelpie
will rise up and snuff out one or more of the nine burning
candles; but if all is well, and the answer is a happy one,
the water spirit will cause the flames to be reflected so
that images play in the water like laughing undines, and not
one of the candles will go out.

☆

When you have done, thank the water spirit and empty the
bowl over a budding rosebush.

☆

As is the usual case, it is best to try this spell at the rising
of the full moon, Freya's moon.

WAX CANDLE *Lovespell*

Light a candle of beeswax, in any quarter of the
moon, but always after dark on a clear starlit night. Take a
pin and stick it gently through the heart of the candle,
right through the wick. Murmur this charm and repeat it
as you work:

*"It's not alone this candle I stick
But my true love's heart I mean to prick;
Whether he be asleep or awake
I'll have him come to me and speak."*

If the pin holds fast in the wick even after the candle has
burnt below the point of insertion, your lover will
appear before you of a certainty; but if the pin falls, it is a
sign that his heart is faithless, and you would do well to
refuse him as a husband.

A WEDDING RING & TUMBLER
Marriage Spell

☆

Maids who wish to find out how soon they are to be
married may work this spell on 28th September, which is
St Michael's Eve.

☆

Light a candle and pass a borrowed wedding ring through
it three times three, to bless it. Then take a hair from your
own head and tie it to the ring; suspend it within a glass
tumbler and blow out the candle, intoning a wish that your
divination may be accurate. (This prayer can be made to
the spirit of the flame or to St Michael.)

☆

Observe the number of times the ring strikes the sides of
the tumbler without being touched or encouraged, and it
will tap out the number of years that will have to pass
away before you make your wedding feast.

The Road
Across the
Ferny Brae

From time immemorial, people all over the world have
spoken of witnessing the fairy revels. It would be strange
indeed to assume that every single one of these millions of
testaments was false!

Britain is particularly rich in reported sightings of the
fairies. Our wiselore teaches that the fairies work under the
instructions of greater beings or angels to direct the life-
force and shape it into herbs, flowers and trees.

Although fairies delight in assuming human form, and not
always in miniature, they are etheric beings, and we
can seldom see them with our bodily eyes: but if we seek
spiritually to enter into the still heart of the natural
world, especially at the breaking of dawn, at noon, in the
evening or under the full moon, we may begin to
perceive them, either busy with their work or merrymaking.
Fairies are very good at merrymaking! They are always
joyful and playful.

☆

Fairies are fascinated by human beings, especially human
love and lovers, but they also fear and resent us – with
good reason – for we are busy destroying their precious
natural world and slaughtering its magic. So we must seek

to commune with them most respectfully, almost reverently! *Feeling* is by far the most important aspect of communication with the fairies. When attempting it, try to enter into harmony with their world and try to feel their ecstatic joy as they go about their tasks . . . and always seek to observe them from the corners of your eyes – for if we turn the full glare of our crude and cramped consciousness upon such delicate and refined creatures, they will disappear in a flash!

☆

One of our most important folklore heroes is "True Thomas", who meets the Queen of Elfland. She points out to him three roads: the first, "thick beset with thorns and briar", is the road belonging to righteousness; the second "lies across the lily leaven" and is the road of wickedness; the Queen then says to Thomas:

☆

"Do you see yon bonny, bonny road
That stretches o'er the ferny brae?
That is the road to fair Elfland,
Where you and I this night must away!"

☆

This ancient rhyme seems to teach us that the true path is the middle path which holds the wise and positive balance between "good" and "evil" – a middle course of good sense and equilibrium.

☆

To work the nature spells which follow, try to attune your mind gently to the divinity and magic inherent in nature – and to the fairy folk. With the right kind of effort, perhaps you will begin to see them! Perhaps, too, they can show us, in these off-balance times, how to find the "road across the ferny brae".

The BIRTHDAY *Marriage Spell*

☆

A spell to be worked upon your birthday is the charm of
the magic laurel, which is to be undertaken thus: rise
between three and four of the clock upon the morning
which is your anniversary, and go secretly and silently into
the garden. There pluck a sprig of laurel, asserting aloud
that it is your birthday and offering the bush your thanks
for the gift. Bear it to your chamber, hold it for three
minutes over some lighted brimstone, measuring the time
on the clockface. Fold the laurel into a fair white linen
cloth in company with a slip of paper upon which are
inscribed your name and that of your suitor, joined with
the sketch of a lover's knot – or, if you have many
admirers, each name. Include also the day of the week,
the date of the year, the age of the moon, and the hour of
the day. Lastly, inscribe the name of the zodiacal star
constellation which presided over the time of your birth.
Then go quickly and bury the packet in the garden, so you
have put it into the underworld, where it must not be
disturbed for three days and three nights. Then you may
take it up, and place it cleanly wrapped in paper beneath
your pillow for three nights, whereupon you will dream
strange and prophetic dreams of wisdom and secrets,
garnered from the underworld kingdoms and the fairy halls.
You will see who is to be your true love, and whether you
are to be married; and much more besides.

The MIDSUMMER MAN *Spell*

☆

Go out by the first bright July moon and gather a stalk of barleycorn as soon as the church clock has struck twelve. You must also gather at this magic hour the herbs rue and camomile and lavender from the garden, the flowers of St John's wort, and a wild rose, for that is a flower truly blessed. This posy of herbs and wild flowers will possess divers magical properties.

☆

Take a small clod of clay, and on putting it into an earthenware vessel, stand the stalk of barleycorn upright in it. Now scatter your posy round the vessel, saying to the barleycorn stalk the while:

☆

"Midsummer Man, Midsummer Man,
With coat so green and beard so wan,
Dreams and wisdom belong to you,
Work your magic the long night through.

Midsummer Man, Midsummer Man,
Tell me, as I know you can,
Shall true-love and wedlock my years span?"

☆

Gather your posy up again, and place it beneath your pillow; then go to bed, and the Midsummer Man, ministered to by the fairies, will work the spell. Remember that the barleycorn in the pot is your Midsummer Man, for you have made him with the powers in your soul. You will do well to treat him with grave respect, because his magic can influence the tide of events, and bring you your heart's desire. You can read the answer to your question the next morning in the way the stalk in the pot is leaning. To the right means yes; to the left, no.

MIDSUMMER EVE *Lovespell*

☆

To work this spell you must fast all Midsummer Eve, and
at night lay a clean cloth of white lace, worked by
maidens, upon the table under a window by which you can
espy the silvery moon. Working only by the moon's light,
spread bread, cheese and ale on the board, then sit down as
if about to make your repast – leaving the front door
open. Then the person destined to be your life's true love
will come into the room as a phantasm, drink to you with
a curtsey or a bow, refill your glass and offer it to you,
bow or curtsey a second time, and then disappear.

The CLOVER LEAF *Lovespell*

☆

Pluck a clover's leaf from white or purple flowers, and
follow the counsel of this spell:

☆

"A clover, a clover of two,
Put it into your right or left shoe;
The first man or woman you meet
In the field, lane or street,
You'll love him or her, or one of his or her name."

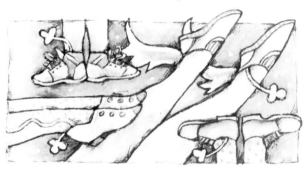

The FOX'S WEDDING *Lovespell*

☆

If a spatter of raindrops fall suddenly out of blue summer
skies, and the shower be over almost before it began, as if
an angel had let fall half a handful of silver from heaven,
old lore states that it betokens a fox's wedding, and that it
is the fairies who bring the rain by magic to honour it.
Such a "marriage of foxes" is very lucky for maidens in
love, and a wish may be made at that time by all.

KING OF THE FAIRIES *Midsummer Spell*

☆

This spell must be worked on Midsummer's Eve or by the light of the shining harvest moon. It must be done as the summer dusk steals away and the dew begins to fall.

☆

Take from the garden a red rose which is full-blown and about to spill its petals. Carry it into the house and scatter the petals about the floor so that they fall like crimson tears, for they are signatures of the heart. Be sure to leave the house door open, so that the moon and the stars may be seen, for you need the breath of their magic.

☆

Then take a clear glass bowl, and fill it up with water from a well or spring, which you will have waiting in a jug. Put it in the middle of the floor, and retire to a dark corner of the room, chanting this charm three times:

☆

"King of the Fairies, ease my soul,
Show my true love's face in this crystal bowl;
Let his heart with me abide,
By this year's end let me be his bride."

☆

By and by you will see a stirring and a faint flutter of the rose petals, as if a little breeze lifted them; and the King of the Fairies will come and dance and make great sport with his folk around the bowl. When all is still, light a white candle and you will see in the bowl the face of the man whose heart you wish to win. If it is smiling, your wish has been granted; if it is frowning, he will never be yours.

☆

If you are asking for the love of a stranger you have yet to meet, his initials will be traced in the rose petals on the floor, as if by a ghostly hand.

MIDSUMMER ASH LEAF *Spell*

☆

This is a lovespell for Midsummer's Eve, which comes down to us from ancient days. Pluck a leaf from the ash, which is a fairy tree, and softly repeat this incantation:

☆

"This green ash leaf in my hand,
The first I meet shall be my man."

☆

Then put it inside your glove and say:

☆

"This green ash leaf in my glove
The first I meet shall be my love."

☆

Place it last of all within your bosom, intoning:

☆

"This green ash leaf within my bosom
The first I meet will be my husband."

☆

Shortly after the working of these spells, your husband will appear to you in a mysterious and magical way – as a ghost by your side, or a face in a mirror or a pool, or a figure in a dream or a vision; and soon after this augury, he will cross the path of your life in person.

The ROSEBUD *Marriage Spell*

☆

Peep out of your window at dawn on a fine summer's morning when all is still and behold the first full-blown rose that you see, then go outside and count the rosebuds clustered just underneath it. The number of buds in the spray tells how many years are to pass before you are wed to your true love.

The TOADSTONE Lovespell

☆

On Midsummer's Eve or Midsummer's Night, or on any
beautiful night of the year, especially when the moon
is full, you may offer a gift to the fairies. This, if it is done
with a sincere heart, is a sure way to win their confidence
and favour.

☆

Bake a little oaten cake, or sew a miniature hood and cape,
or, better still, offer the fairies a song or a dance or a
verse that you have made up, or that you find pleasing. Say
aloud before you begin the work: "This is for the fairies",
and let the gift be given out of doors in a sequestered
place, wild and lonely.

☆

Then, very soon, most likely the next day, you will
find that the fairies give something back to you; keep your
eyes sharp for their gift, but let not your giving be done
because you think that such a gift will be given in return,
neither expect anything; keep a look-out for it, all
the same. It is certain that very soon you will find some
curious but lovely object from nature, or you may
find some silver money. Whatever you find, keep it for
ever, because that is a sacred gift, and will bring you
good luck and happiness.

☆

Most often the item you will find will be a toadstone – a
round pebble with mysterious and beautiful mottlings and
marks, seeming to glow with many delicate hues. Keep this
by you, and sleep with it under your pillow; according
to wiselore, these stones are the mystic jewel that is to be
found in the head of the toad. She (or he) who holds
such a stone will be lucky in love, wise in divination, and
blessed in life.

68

The OAK LEAF *Spell*

☆

If a maid that is deep in love goes with her suitor to a
lonely place in the meadows or the woods, or to the
moors, and places within her own and her lover's shoe a
single oak leaf; and if they both wait there and contemplate
their love, and speak it one to another as evening falls
and the stars come out, they will, if their patience is good,
behold the fairy host as they come to gambol and sport
in the wilds.

The PEAPOD *Marriage Spell*

☆

Unmarried damsels may discover how soon they will wed
by searching for a peapod whose wallet holds nine peas,
neither more nor less, and pinning it up over the street
door. If the first visitor to enter the house afterwards be a
single man, she may be sure that she will marry, or be
betrothed, within the year.

The FAIRY PIPER *Lovespell*

☆

If any young swain should find himself in a secluded place
out in the wilds, and quite lonely, upon midsummer
morning, and should hear the sound of the fairy pipes as
dawn breaks and the sun rises, that will put a spell on him.
He will be fated to take a fairy wife, who will bring him
much discovery and joy, wonder and delight, and much
consternation and sorrow, for he must lose her; yet he will
dream ever after of her, and no mortal woman will take
her place; and he shall have children by the fairy wife, and
prosper; and he will not be able to escape his fate,
howsoever he dreads it; for he also longs for it. There is no
way to break the spell, or see it die.

The MYRTLE *Marriage Spell*

☆

Let a number of fair damsels, not less than three and not more than seven, gather together privately and secretly at night in a room where they will not be disturbed, perfect silence being observed by all, just as the clock strikes eleven. Each one must bring forth from her breast a sprig of myrtle, which she has worn there all day, folded up in a scrap of tissue paper.

☆

A small chafing-dish of charcoal is to be ignited, and on it each maiden casts nine hairs from her head and a paring of her toe and fingernails. Then she blesses the myrtle with a charm of her own which she has created herself, having learned it by heart. All the while that she is weaving the charm, she must sprinkle a few drops of frankincense and lavender oil upon the charcoal.

As the aromatic vapour ascends, the myrtle sprig is steeped in its fragrant fumes, and the magic spirit which is in all nature will rise up in power.

☆

The damsels then retire to bed exactly as the clock strikes the mystic hour of twelve, each placing the myrtle beneath her pillow and adjuring it to speak to her of her lover in her dreams. They may fall into slumber assured that they will dream of their future marriage partner.

The DANDELION *Marriage Spell*

☆

Find a dandelion whose seeds are ripe, and pluck it gently.
Blow away its feathery clock, and count the number of
breaths you use to do so; that is the number of years which
must fly away like summer birds before you greet your
wedding-morning.

The KERN BABY

☆

The Kern Baby is a little doll made of the last stalks of
corn to be harvested in the field. If a maid makes one and
washes it in the dew of the grass, which wise folk say is the
sweat of the stars, upon the night of the next new moon's
crescent, in the early hours, then hangs it over her bed, she
will ensure for herself a happy and speedy marriage, rosy-
cheeked bairns, and a life full of wisdom and learning.

The FAIRY THIMBLES *Lovespell*

☆

A young maid who goes out and looks for the first
harebells of spring, which are called "fairy thimbles" and are
witches' flowers, and then counts them up, will know the
number of years which must pass in procession before she
can hope for marriage. If there are a great number, she
must count backwards from twelve and walk in a circle
widdershins (anticlockwise); and therefore may hope for a
better destiny. Let her not harm any of the flowers in
her perambulation; and let her, after her business is
through, address the fairies thus:

☆

"Fairies, I have sought your bower;
I now retire, and bless your power."

☆

She must then bow three times to the fairies, and the magic
of the glade will go with her.

The MOONLIT CORNFIELD *Lovespell*

☆

If you wish to know the secrets of love and the mysteries, you must be bold of heart and go by night, at the time of the full moon nearest to Midsummer's Day, into the middle of a cornfield which is in its first flush of gold. Take care not to harm any of the cornstalks as you go.

☆

You must wait with a quiet spirit at the field's heart, training your mind upon the full shining moon. Before long the fairies and other nature beings will make their

appearance, and if they find you worthy, will impart to you their wisdom and visions. Beware of the terror falling upon you, for this is sure to aggravate the fairies. If you can withstand the terror, you will be much favoured by them all the days of your life, and the knowledge they teach you will grow and grow, like a king's treasure-store.

☆

When you are ready to come away from the cornfield, bow to the moon and bless the fairies, remembering to offer your thanks; then you may be sure that unseen friends will walk with you on your way home.

The ROSE LEAF *Marriage Spell*

☆

This is a useful spell for a young maiden who has many
men wishing to court her, and is undecided in her heart as
to whom to choose from the company. She must pluck
fresh rose leaves according to the number of her suitors,
and, having given each leaf the name of a lover, must
scatter them upon the ground by throwing them up into
the air. The last leaf to settle would be the one best
for her to marry, for wedlock with him would bring her
happiness, prosperity of the world and of the soul; so
speak the rose leaves.

The HERB *Marriage Spell*

☆

Take a sprig of red sage, a sprig of rosemary or any other
fragrant garden herb, and place it in a glass jar with two
other aromatic herbs of the wilderness. Keep the sprigs
upright and supported by the sides of the jar. Now break
up one ounce of cinnamon into fine pieces, and mix it with
two ounces of frankincense and six drops of cassia oil. Put
this compound into the jar, in the middle of the
surrounding herbs whose stems must be bent so that they
form a delicate fairy bower over the incense.

☆

When all is done, go out and bury the jar under an apple
tree, having first stopped the mouth with parchment. Upon
retiring and rising, do not fail to utter this rune:

☆

"O fragrant herbs, I ask of thee
That my chosen one might love me;
May he seek a happy life
And make of me his wedded wife."

☆

Do not approach the jar in any wise, until you have
married your own true love, or the spell will die away.

Two LOVE POTIONS

It is part of our folk heritage that herbs and all growing
things bear associations and correspondences with the
moon, the planets and the "stars of the firmament".
Wiselore teaches that all things in creation are in
harmonious sympathy with one another, and that it is for us
to try to understand and appreciate this deep union.

☆

The herbs that are given for use in the love philtres or
potions are anciently associated with Venus, the planet of
beauty, love and the arts. Some have long been in use, too,
as herbs which increase our faculties for psychic wisdom
and apperception. Alchemists, wisewomen and sorcerers of
old used these herbs to help their development.

☆

You should never seek to force or demand that your
desired partner should fall in love with you, because that is
an interference with free will! When magic is used in an
attempt to intervene in this way, it becomes black magic,
for the intention is not pure. White magic does not
force or demand; instead, it gives aid and blessing to our
hopes and endeavours. If it is right that our wishes
should be fulfilled, it assures that the most favourable
and beneficent spiritual atmosphere will be provided
for this to come to pass.

☆

Use the potion as either a tisane (a tea) or use it for
bathing, especially the face and the eyes. Feel that the herbs

79

are imparting their Venus qualities of wisdom and magic to you (some of the herbs are of the moon and Neptune). The potion is for you alone – it is not necessary to induce your hoped-for lover to take the tea!

☆

If in your own soul you can contact and absorb the soul-qualities of the herbs and the magic you create in concocting them under the mystery of the tranquil full moon, or at that "holy time when the day breaks but the sun has not yet risen, and the whole world is new-born", you could well be successful in your endeavours!

☆

As, for the purposes of the first spell, you should "finish the potion" at midnight, it might be a good idea to avoid making too much of it! And if you have a delicate palate, you may be pleased to know that bathing offers another way of using any love potion. If you do choose this method, however, drink just a little of the philtre too, as there is no better way to draw close to the essence of a sympathetic herb than to taste it!

☆

Pour the potion into the bath, which should be prepared either at six o'clock in the evening or at midnight, according to your convenience, for three consecutive days after the working of the love-potion spell; and, as the wisewoman says, "make of it a sacred experience".

☆

Then there is nothing to do but to wait till the coming of the next full moon, since by then the spell should have cast its influence.

The WHITE WITCH'S *Love Potion*

☆

The flowers and fragrant herbs needed to brew a love potion are the flowers of shining Venus and the full moon. They must be gathered at first light, and you should finish your task before the flush of sunrise has paled from the skies; the herbs must be counted nine times, and plucked from nine different places.

Gather a few leaves of the blackberry bush, cowslip flowers and elder flowers, fennel, meadowsweet, mint and mayblossom, violets, watercress and sorrel. If some of these have finished flowering, then gather at least the leaves; and if you cannot find some of the plants, it is permitted that you may obtain a little of the dried herb from a wisewoman or some old wife skilled in the arts of wortcunning. Keep these in bags of fresh white linen until the morning of your great enterprise; but be sure to gather some of the leaves and flowers with your own hand, or the philtre will fail in potency.

☆

At the stroke of six, you must infuse the herbs in boiling water drawn from a pure stream. Pour the water over them and let them stand to cool. Use earthenware or a strong glass bowl, but never an iron vessel, because this would break the spell. Take out the leaves after two minutes, but you may leave behind any flowers or petals to float in the infusion.

☆

You must drink a little of the potion throughout the day,

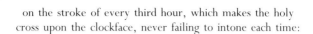

on the stroke of every third hour, which makes the holy
cross upon the clockface, never failing to intone each time:

☆

"St Agnes, bright Venus, and Sweet Lady Moon,
Bring my heart's best beloved to my side very soon;
This brew that I drink is your magic key
And if it is meet then so mote it be."

At midnight you must finish the potion, drinking every last
drop to hail the moon. Then you must bow solemnly
to the silvery orb nine times, and walk backwards to bed,
where you will sleep soundly.

☆

Before the next moon, if it is right, your chosen lover will
certainly be courting you.

The MISTLETOE *Dreaming Philtre*

☆

It is said that an unmarried maid who gathers mistletoe leaves under the bright shining of Freya's full moon, and at midnight steeps them in a liquid composed of equal parts of wine, cider vinegar and honey, taking this after a fast of three hours, and then proceeding to bed, will be sure to dream of her future husband.

☆

On waking you should quickly note down, while you remember, the descriptions of any mythological beasts or magical creatures you saw or heard in your dreams, for these will indicate the characteristics and qualities you must look for in your future spouse. If the beings spoke to you, expect these intimated qualities to be of an ordinary everyday kind such as are found in most men; but if the dream-creatures were heard to sing, then you may rejoice indeed, for your promised mate will be blessed with great virtues of the heart.

☆

If you do not understand the message you have received, you need not be troubled by it; all will be made clear in the fullness of time; only be sure not to try to work this spell without taking a little paper and ink to put by your bedside for use on waking.

☆

If you have a desired sweetheart in mind, you must speak his name three times before you drop off to sleep; and then the dream-creatures will come either to warn you or to confirm the wisdom of your choice; and in the latter case, it will usually come to pass that your cherished one will be with you by the waning of the next full moon.

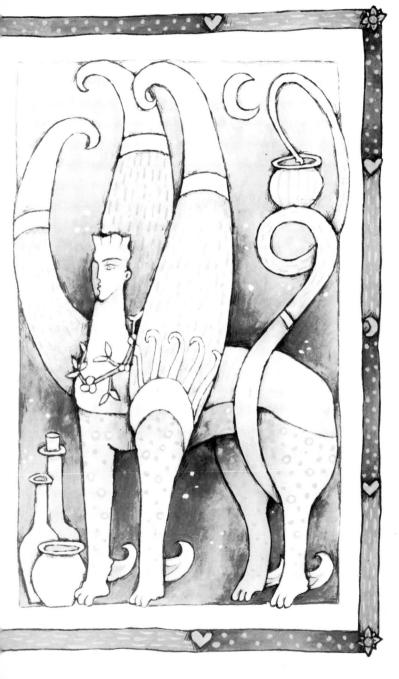

Glossary

☆

MAYBLOSSOM *Crataegus oxyacantha* White blossom of the hawthorn (a small thorny tree) which appears in May

ROWAN TREE *Sorbus aucuparia* The mountain-ash, which bears red berries in the summer

YELLOW ARCHANGEL *Lamiastrum galeobdolon* Sometimes called the yellow dead-nettle, this trailing plant has leaves similar in appearance to the stinging nettle, but bears vivid yellow flowers

RUE *Ruta graveolens* The green leaves of this aromatic herb have a sheen of blue-grey, and the flowers are yellow-green

BARLEYCORN *Hordeum sativum* A stalk of barley with its gold-white 'beard'

HAREBELL *Campanula rotundifolia* Perennial wild campanula with thin wiry stems and blue bell-like flowers (the Sottish bluebell)

COWSLIP *Primula officinalis* A species of primrose with light green leaves and yellow flowers (commonly called the 'keys of heaven')

ELDERFLOWER *Sambucus* The blossom of the elder, growing in white umbel-sprays with a sharp, distinctive, bittersweet fragrance

MEADOWSWEET *Filipendula ulmaria* Flourishes in damp meadows and ditches, its creamy yellow flowers which grow in tall, delicate starry clusters exuding a sweet, heady scent

SORREL *Acetosa* Its long green leaves creep upward along the stem, culminating in a point, and its flowers are small, tight-clustered, and red in colour

KALE *Brassica oleracea* A cabbage-like vegetable with curled, wrinkled leaves of a deep green colour

MANDRAKE *Mandragoras* A low-growing Oriental narcotic plant, a member of the potato family, with a large fleshy forked root, often resembling the shape of a man or woman

LIST OF SPELLS

☆